GRACE LETTERS

Practical Steps to Experiencing
Transformation through Forgiveness

EMILY A. EDWARDS, PH.D.

LIVING HOPE PUBLISHING
Midland, Texas

LIVING HOPE PUBLISHING
www.LivingHopePublishing.com

Book design by TLC Graphics, *www.TLCGraphics.com*
Cover: Tamara Dever, Interior: Erin Stark

Dove photo: © Depositphotos.com/JuliaSha

Forgiveness by Matthew West
Used by Permission. All Rights Reserved.
Atlas Music Publishing

Unless otherwise noted, all Scripture quotations are taken from the New King James Version®. Copyright © 1982 by Thomas Nelson, Inc. Used by permission. All rights reserved.

Some concepts adapted from materials published by Victorious Christian Living International, 14900 W. Van Buren Street, Goodyear, AZ 85338. Copyright © 2006 VCLi, Version 2.0 Used by permission. All rights reserved.

ISBN: 978-0-9816709-6-6

CONTENTS

Appendix

ACKNOWLEDGMENTS

First and foremost, I would like to thank my Lord and Savior, Jesus Christ, who has made me who I am today. Thank you for saving my soul. It is Your love and forgiveness that motivates me to share my heart and the topic of forgiveness with others.

I would like to thank my husband, Chad, for your patience, love, and support through this journey.

I would specifically like to thank the VCLi staff for allowing me to use their forgiveness diagrams and principles to share this message. I would also like to thank Fred and Valerie Paine for working with me on this project.

I would like to thank the following people for their work and contributions toward this book: Heidi Tolliver Walker, Morgan MacDonald, Jenny Mertes, Tamara Dever, Erin Stark, Steven Brown, Cathy Kessler, and Kristen Brown.

Last, but not least, I would like to thank all of my family and friends who always love and support me.

INTRODUCTION

Have the words and actions of others left you wounded and scarred? Do you lay awake at night, thinking about *that moment*— that moment when your world was turned upside-down? We've all experienced it. The offense against us plays over and over in our minds. When anything happens that reminds us of *that moment*, we replay it in our heads, act out, lash out, and withdraw.

Day after day, month after month, and year after year, we yearn for freedom from the pain and suffering that weighs heavy on our minds, emotions, and even our bodies. We try earnestly to forget, but soon discover that erasing those memories is as impossible as sweeping the sand from the seashore or blotting the stars from the night sky.

We fantasize about our offenders groveling before us, acknowledging their wrongdoing and pleading for our forgiveness. We think, *They must suffer for what they did! They must pay!* We want revenge.

Many people have tried revenge as a means of freeing themselves from suffering, only to discover they are still chained to their pain. Even worse, they drown in their bitterness, which taints their relationships and drives away even those they love. The writer of Hebrews says, "Looking carefully lest anyone fall short of the grace of God; lest any root of bitterness springing up cause trouble, and by this many become defiled" (Hebrews 12:15).

The moment of offense knocks over the first in a long series of connected events. Like a line of dominoes, it topples our emotional wellbeing, our relationships, our physical health, and every detail of our daily lives. It even hinders our fellowship with God. Eventually, we find ourselves locked in a *prison of unforgiveness*, while the offender seems to be off the hook. From a human perspective, it seems completely unfair.

The answer to complete healing isn't "getting over it." It isn't trying to forget, getting revenge, or simply waiting for time to pass. The key to freedom, from the smallest offense to the most horrific, is forgiveness. In Matthew 6:14-15, Jesus says, "For if you forgive men their trespasses, your heavenly Father will also forgive you. But if you do not forgive men their trespasses, neither will your Father forgive your trespasses."

To experience the healing and freedom that comes from forgiveness, we must choose to forgive, even if the offender doesn't deserve it—just as Jesus chose to forgive us. You might protest by saying, "But I don't *feel* like forgiving!" There's good news! Forgiveness is not an emotion. It is a choice. We don't have to *feel* like forgiving in order to forgive. The Bible says, "Bearing with one another, and forgiving one another, if anyone has a complaint against another; even as Christ forgave you, so you also must do" (Colossians 3:13).

When we choose to forgive, we unlock the door of our prison and leave behind our emotional pain, mental torment, and bitterness.

Like you, I have been deeply hurt. When I was young, I was belittled and rejected because I suffered from epilepsy. Both as a child and an adult, I was sexually, verbally, and physically abused. For many years, I didn't know how to truly and fully forgive. I agonized in my own prison of unforgiveness. When I was at my lowest point, God took my hand and led me out.

In *Grace Letters: Practical Steps to Experiencing Transformation through Forgiveness*, I share the keys to freedom based on biblical principles and Victorious Christian Living International's discipleship curriculum. I, and thousands of fellow prisoners, have used these keys to be set free.

This book, while told as a fictional story, clarifies what forgiveness is and what it is not. It outlines the four keys of forgiveness, why it is vital to forgive, and how to forgive. At the end, you will find a 21-Day Forgiveness Challenge, which lists twenty-one steps you can take to be set free from your prison of unforgiveness. I hope you will use these tools to forgive those who have hurt and offended you and find complete healing and freedom—forever.

You, too, can be set free from the prison of unforgiveness that enslaves you!

Chapter One

IMPRISONED BY UNFORGIVENESS

Tiny, white cracks of light crawled up the stone wall, reminding Grace how dark it was inside her prison. She kept her breaths shallow, not wanting to fill her lungs with the stale air. She couldn't remember how many times she had scrubbed the walls with bleach, only to have the moldy smell return. She tried to gag down a few bites of her tasteless evening meal. In disgust, she slid the metal tray across the cement floor toward the cell bars, and the screeching sound made her cringe, as if someone were scraping their nails slowly down a chalkboard. Grace slumped over onto her cot and began scratching at the persistent rash that covered her arms and neck. All five of her senses were being assaulted at once. *I wish I were dead*, she thought.

Grace closed her eyes, longing for a peaceful night's sleep, but she knew this night would be no different from the others. Since *that moment*, she had been tormented by fitful dreams and awoken each morning, soaked in perspiration. Each sunrise brought throbbing headaches and knots in her stomach. Her nights were haunted, but her days weren't much better. She was besieged by the constant onslaught of emotions—anger, hurt, fear, confusion, and loneliness. *Why am I here?* she asked the unrelenting silence.

Grace picked up a piece of rock, fallen from her prison wall, and etched in the wall the word *basanizo*, the Greek word for "torment," over and over again. It was something she learned in school, but now basanizo lived with her, taunting her every waking moment.

Why am I the one being punished? she demanded of the empty walls. As she traced the final "o" again, her ruthless grip on the rock tightened. *He's going to pay*, she vowed.

Over the years, Grace had called friends, family, and spiritual leaders—anyone who would listen—but no one could offer her satisfactory answers. For a while, they had commiserated: "You poor thing. He needs to pay!" But as time went on, their comments had become calloused: "You need to get over it, Grace. Good grief! Are you still bringing all that up?" After a while, she had quit calling. Nobody wanted to hear her sob story for the thousandth time. Now the phone was silent. *Silent as the grave*, she thought, as she took refuge behind the four gray steel bars of her tiny prison cell.

As she lay looking up at the ceiling, trying to count the bubbles in the cement, she thought back to the days before *that moment*. She'd been happy and free; now, she thought, *I wish I could be free again.* She'd slept well back then in her comfy bed, waking to the early rays of sun filtering through her bedroom shutters. She'd felt close to her friends and family, and to God. Now, these walls shut out everyone and everything.

Suddenly, she heard the heavy footsteps of the jailer echoing through the hallway. It was time to make sure all the prisoners were locked securely away. Grace pulled the thin, yellowed sheet over her head for protection. *Haven't I been tormented enough?* she asked herself. *I can't stand another moment in this place. I've got to get out of here!*

That moment was like a horror movie that played daily in the theater of her mind. She'd sit through it white-knuckled each time, hoping somehow the ending would change and the good guy would win for once.

At first, she'd liked those steel bars. They seemed to protect her from further pain, but now those tall sentinels were as unwanted as a case of the shingles. She'd had shingles before, and it had been extremely painful. The doctor had told her if the condition wasn't treated quickly, it could cause permanent nerve damage, creating an agony that could only be managed with regular doses of morphine. *Ah, for an overdose of morphine to quiet the pain in my soul…to drift into oblivion*, she thought.

Grace sat bolt upright. "No!" she declared out loud. "I want to live." She shot up, grabbed her metal tray, and began beating it against the bars, yelling, "Someone has to pay for what he did to me! Who's going to pay?" Angry tears streamed down her face. Her energy spent, she slid down the bars to the floor and began wiping the tears from her cheeks.

I'm exhausted, she thought, as she let her head lean against the bars. In desperation, Grace cried out, *Lord, I want to be free of this prison of torment. Please help me!*

She reached up and took her Bible from the edge of her cot. She let it flop open to no place in particular. A folded piece of paper, perhaps from a Bible study long ago, dropped from its pages onto the floor beside her.

It was a letter, addressed to her.

Dear Grace,

Here are four keys I have given you to be free from your past and unlock your future.

As Grace read the letter, time seemed to stand still. Here, tucked into the pages of God's Word, was what God had been asking her to do all along.

When someone commits an offense against you, it is tempting to refuse to forgive them, especially when the wound is deep. However, when you refuse to forgive, you become the prisoner, not the offender. You are the one who ends up trapped in the prison of unforgiveness.

The author had sketched out a diagram that grabbed her attention.

PRISON OF UNFORGIVENESS

The Offense

The Hurt

My Sinful Reactions

Ramifications

As Grace stared at the diagram, she caught her breath. *Hey, that's me!*

The prison of unforgiveness has four bars. The first is the offense. This is what the person did or did not do to hurt you. The second bar of the prison is the hurt. This is how you felt as a result of that offense. You may have felt betrayed, embarrassed, rejected, belittled, unimportant, depressed, angry, or devastated.

Yes! Grace thought. *That's exactly how I feel. Yes! Yes! Yes!*

The third bar of the prison is the ramifications of the offense. This is how the offense affected your life afterwards. The fourth bar of the prison is your sinful reactions. These are the wrong choices you made as a result of the offense.

But there is good news! You hold the keys to your freedom. To break free of this prison, here is what you need to do:

PRISON OF UNFORGIVENESS

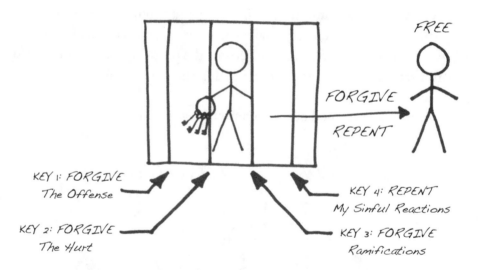

Grace stared at the letter. Her eyes were drawn to the image of the keys. Then she looked at the image of the person outside the prison—free.

Folded behind the letter was a stack of blank paper. Grace took one of the sheets and laid it in front of her. Gently, she put her pen to the paper, and titled it: "Key #1: The Offense." But where to start? Jake wasn't the only one whose choices had scarred her, but his were the most recent. She thought back to *that moment* and shuddered. She listed every way Jake had hurt her. Her tears began to flow.

When she finished that list, Grace took a deep breath, trying to relax the tightness she felt in her chest. She turned to a blank piece of paper and wrote at the top "Key #2: The Hurt." She listed every emotion that had torn at her heart because of Jake's offense.

Next, "Key #3: Ramifications." She detailed each negative consequence that came into her life since *that moment*. Her writing went on and on until her head, heart, and hand ached.

Finally, she took another piece of paper and wrote "Key #4: My Sinful Reactions." At first, Grace couldn't think what to write. She hadn't sinned, had she? She prayed for God's wisdom. Gradually, she began to see her time in this prison of unforgiveness in a different light. She slowly wrote out her reactions to *that moment* that were tainted with anger, bitterness, selfishness, and ultimately unforgiveness.

She stared at her lists. Breathing was becoming easier now, yet something nagged at her. Another name was coming to mind. She took out another sheet of paper and started a new list. Grace suspected it might not be the last.

Several hours later, she was surrounded by pages full of lists. She closed her eyes, exhausted.

A Few Hours Later

When Grace opened her eyes the door to the prison cell was open. Could it be? *If this is a dream, I don't want to wake up,* she thought. She looked around, but she was alone. With the keys in her hand, she stepped out and took a deep breath of fresh air. Like a dream, the walls evaporated. The damp smell drifted away, the fog lifted from her mind, and suddenly she was standing in the hallway of her cozy little home. Her head twisted in every direction, making her almost trip as she made her way down the hall to her kitchen.

Oh, for a glass of freshly brewed sweet tea, she thought. It was a simple pleasure, but Grace was going to savor each moment of her newly regained freedom. She heated the water, dropped a teabag into the steaming cup, and followed it with a generous scoop of organic sugar.

As the tea brewed, she turned to open the door that led into the backyard. *It's spring, and I hadn't even noticed,* she thought. *The trees are budding. New life!* She stood on the threshold and realized her headache was gone, and so was the itchy rash. She'd tried every lotion and ointment known to man—

or woman—to get rid of it. What man could not do, God had accomplished in moments. Unforgiveness even caused this? *I once was blind, but now I see.*

As she looked out at her emerald green yard, softly glowing in the last rays of day, she felt she was seeing God's creation for the first time. *Lord, I'm so grateful for freedom. Thank you!* Grace paused, struggling to find just the right words. *That's all I can say—thank you.*

For years, she'd been consumed with her "unjust" imprisonment, wanting her offender to pay for his crimes against her. Now, her thoughts effortlessly turned to others. *How many others are locked away in that dreadful prison? How miserable they must be. Lord, I want to help them find the four keys to true, complete forgiveness, too.*

Chapter Two

GOD'S
GRACE

❧

Grace rolled over on her bed, stretched her arms toward the headboard, and arched her back. *Thank you, Lord, for another night of glorious rest.* The sun was just peeking through the leafy canopy of the live oak trees that graced her tranquil neighborhood. A breeze fluttered the lace curtains. Mockingbirds were beginning their morning repertoire of melodies. She relaxed her back and hugged her white, fluffy comforter. After a glance at the clock on her nightstand, she sighed and swung her legs over the side of her bed and slid her toes into her waiting slippers. Her terrycloth robe lay across the bed like a relaxed soul after a massage. Tying the sash, she thought about *that moment* and breathed a morning prayer: *Thank you for another day of freedom. I'm so grateful You set me free.*

Grace went to the kitchen, pushed the button on her coffee machine for a double shot, and grabbed the cream from the fridge. She watched the coffee drip into her favorite blue mug, and turn into a luscious caramel color as she mixed in the cream. She lifted the mug to her lips and savored the first delicious sip as she settled into her overstuffed "prayer chair." She kicked off her slippers, folded her legs under her robe, and picked up her Bible to begin her daily devotions.

Today's reading was the parable of the forgiving king and the unforgiving servant from Matthew 18:23–35:

Therefore the kingdom of heaven is like a certain king who wanted to settle accounts with his servants. And when he had begun to settle accounts, one was brought to him who owed him ten thousand talents. But as he was not able to pay, his master commanded that he be sold, with his wife and children and all that he had, and that payment be made. The servant therefore fell down before him, saying, "Master, have patience with me, and I will pay you all." Then the master of that servant was moved with compassion, released him, and forgave him the debt.

But that servant went out and found one of his fellow servants who owed him a hundred denarii; and he laid hands on him and took him by the throat, saying, "Pay me what you owe!" So his fellow servant fell down at his feet and begged him, saying, "Have patience with me, and I will pay you all." And he would not, but went and threw him into prison till he should pay the debt.

So when his fellow servants saw what had been done, they were very grieved, and came and told their master all that had been done. Then his master, after he had called him, said to him, "You wicked servant! I forgave you all that debt because you begged me. Should you not also have had compassion on your fellow servant, just as I had pity on you?" And his master was angry, and delivered him to the torturers until he should pay all that was due to him.

So My heavenly Father also will do to you if each of you, from his heart, does not forgive his brother his trespasses.

Grace closed her Bible and exhaled, not realizing she'd been holding her breath the whole time. The truth conveyed in this parable was indeed accurate. She had experienced it firsthand. *Thank you, Jesus, for forgiving my enormous debt to You, my sins and disobedience. You were merciful to me, even though I refused to forgive my offender right away. Instead, I chose to hold onto bitterness that kept me stuck for years in the prison of unforgiveness. You allowed me to come to the end of myself so that the only one I could turn to for deliverance was You. When I forgave Jake's debt, You set me free.*

Later that morning, Grace went outside to check the mailbox. She received a letter, and took note of the return address. *Oh, good, another one,* she thought. In the left-hand corner of the envelope, the writer had scrawled, "Prisoner Paine."

Grace carried the letter into her home office and sat down in the gray leather chair at her desk. She reached for her letter opener, a miniature replica of the double-edged Roman sword described by the Apostle Paul in Ephesians 6. She started to slide the blade under the sealed top of the envelope, then paused. She closed her eyes and prayed the confession she made each day before she began to work:

Heavenly Father,

I pray for my mind. May my mind be renewed and set on You today. May the Holy Spirit bring to my mind everything You have taught me.

I pray for my eyes. May I see myself and others through Your eyes. May I see Your answers clearly. May I see things for what they truly are and not be misled.

I pray for my ears. May I hear Your voice. May I hear people's hearts. May I discern what is truth and what are lies.

I pray for my mouth. May Your words be in my mouth to bring healing, freedom, direction, correction, and encouragement.

I pray for my heart. May my heart be pure before You. May my heart be full of Your love for others. May my heart be satisfied with Your acceptance.

I pray for my hands. May my hands be anointed to touch others with healing and comfort. May my hands be generous and filled with good things.

I pray for my feet. May my feet go where You want me to go. May my feet put me in front of the teachable, the needy, the lost, and the spiritually hungry to present the good news.

Heavenly Father, I dedicate myself to You.

In Jesus' name. Amen.

After her prayer, Grace slid the blade through the top of the envelope and pulled out the letter. She unfolded the sheet of paper; inside was a small picture of the writer. Grace asked the people who contacted her to enclose their pictures. She set the photo aside and began to read.

Dear Dr. Grace,

I heard you on the radio and was hoping you could help me, too. I've been imprisoned since *that moment*—four years, two months, and ten days ago…

Grace stopped reading and picked up the picture. She looked over at the wall in her office where she tacked all of the pictures of her clients and stood up to add this new one. The Freedom Wall was growing.

Chapter Three

FORGIVING
ABUSE

⌒

As she pinned the picture on the wall, Grace studied her newest client, a lovely, blonde twenty-something with piercing blue eyes. Grace continued reading the letter at the point where she had left off earlier:

I was raised in a Christian home, got saved at kids' camp, and took a purity vow at age thirteen.

When I was seventeen, my boyfriend Cliff, who is now my husband, forced me to have sex. I got pregnant, and he talked me into having an abortion. Even though I knew it was wrong, I agreed because I thought being a single mom would ruin my Christian witness and break my parents' hearts.

Later, Cliff and I got married. I'm not sure he really wanted to marry me. I think he felt guilty and was trying to make it up to me. Last year, our baby girl was born on Valentine's Day. I'm now a stay-at-home mom.

At one point, I passionately loved Cliff, but *that moment* drove a huge wedge between us. If there was ever real love there, it's gone. I've survived by focusing on our daughter. Cliff has focused on work, his computer, and a vast quantity of alcohol. There's no communication, and we haven't been to church in years.

I can't stand how selfish and self-centered he is. It's all about him, his wants, and his needs. I'm at the end of my rope and would divorce him if it wasn't for baby Abigail.

11

Please, tell me you can help.

Desperate,

Liri Paine

Grace set down the paper and put her head in her hands. She gently rubbed her temples with her thumbs and breathed deeply, trying to see life through Liri's eyes. She prayed for wisdom and began to pen the following response:

Dear Liri,

Thank you for your letter. I was intrigued by your name because I hadn't heard it before. When I Googled it, I discovered that it's Albanian for "freedom." God wants you free, Liri. Even your name declares it!

I feel compelled to share a personal story with you. I think it will give you hope.

Years ago, I began attending a singles group at my church. One of the leaders was an attractive man named Jake who seemed to love God. I was immediately interested. A few weeks later, he asked me out, and we began dating.

After knowing each other for only two weeks, he proposed. As crazy as it sounds now, I accepted. Not long after the engagement, his true colors began to show. One day, Jake walked in while I was talking on the phone, and he jumped to the conclusion that I was cheating on him. He became enraged and pushed me to the ground. When I tried shaking him off, he grabbed the can of pepper spray he kept by the door and shot it into my eyes. Somehow, I was still able to break away and call the police. They quickly arrived.

In *that moment*, my bitterness, fear, and anger grew into an iron giant, impossible for me to bring down. I broke off the engagement and began to judge men as dangerous, volatile, and dishonest. I became afraid of commitment. What if I made another mistake? I decided that I was not a good judge of character.

The effects of *that moment* contaminated every area of my life— my health, my thinking, my emotions, my relationships, and even my fellowship with the Lord. Although Jake was the one in the wrong, *I* ended up imprisoned by my own bitterness. It didn't seem fair.

For years, I was tormented by painful memories and the sheer terror of *that moment*. I wanted revenge. I wanted him to pay for what he had done.

Ultimately, I learned that unforgiveness imprisons and torments us even more than the original offense. If not dealt with, our unwillingness to forgive affects us for the rest of our lives. Time does not heal all wounds.

Tears of gratitude fill my eyes right now, Liri, as I think about how God's mercy revealed to me this truth: I am set free when I forgive those who have hurt me.

Understandably, I didn't feel like forgiving Jake. I was still angry with him for what he had done, and I wanted him to pay.

Then God showed me that Jesus had already paid. His blood covers all of my sins, your sins, and the sins of those who have sinned against us. As John the Baptist said, "Behold! The Lamb of God who takes away the sin of the world!" (John 1:29)

Even though I didn't feel like forgiving Jake, I realized that I needed to forgive him. I also knew it would require an act of my will. I would have to choose to forgive him, and I would be the one who benefitted the most. In Matthew 6:14, Jesus says, "For if you forgive men their trespasses, your heavenly Father will also forgive you." Through a friend, God showed me the four keys to unlock the prison of unforgiveness.

The first key was to accept the blood of Jesus as the full payment for what my offender had done. I prayed this prayer: *Heavenly Father, I choose to forgive Jake for what he did to me. He attacked me, held me down, and sprayed pepper spray into my eyes. I believe the blood of Jesus covers his offense.*

The second key was to confess the emotions I felt about what he had done. I listed them and prayed this prayer: *Heavenly Father, I choose to forgive Jake for all the emotions I felt regarding this offense. I believe the blood of Jesus covers all these emotions.*

The third key was to confess all the ways *that moment* negatively affected my life afterwards. I wrote down all the ramifications and prayed this prayer: *Heavenly Father, I choose to forgive Jake for all the ramifications of his choices, and how those choices affected my life. I believe the blood of Jesus covers all these ramifications.*

The fourth key was to confess my own sin. I prayed this prayer: *Heavenly Father, I repent of judging and condemning Jake for what he did to me. I believe the blood of Jesus covers my sins, and I thank you that I'm forgiven.*

Grace's pen flew across the page as she explained the four life-changing keys to Liri. With bold strokes, she wrote line upon line the truths God had revealed to her. She knew Liri could be free, too.

After pouring out her heart in the letter, Grace spent time praying for Liri. When she looked up at her clock, it was almost noon. She thought, *I'd better eat something and then start preparing for Bible study tonight.*

Chapter Four

A LIFETIME
OF REGRET

he next morning, Grace heard Burt, the mailman, coming up the front porch steps. She grabbed the letter she had written the day before, shouted a greeting out the window, and asked him to wait while she hurried downstairs.

Burt nodded as he looked at the mail in his hand. "Keep your pen warm, Grace," he hollered back. "I think you have another letter!"

Grace popped out through the front door. "Thanks, Burt," she said. "Here you go." The ingoing and outgoing mail exchanged hands.

"I don't know how you do it," Burt said, looking at the completed letter. "You spend so much time writing letters. How do you fit it all in?"

Grace looked at the new letter in her hands. *I wonder the same thing*, she thought. She loved answering letters, but she was finding it increasingly difficult to balance the demands of her day job with her desire to help others who wrote to her sharing their pain and seeking her help. There was only so much time in the day.

Grace sighed. "I wish I could do more."

"You do a lot more than you think." Burt lifted the letter to his head like a salute and turned to descend the front porch stairs.

"Oh, wait—I almost forgot!" Grace called after him. "I made a cheesecake last night and saved you a piece. Do you have a second for me to run and get it?"

Burt had been her mailman for years, but they had become friends about a year and a half ago, when he asked about all of the letters she was sending. Now, his picture hung on the Freedom Wall, too.

Grace set the stack of mail on the hall table and ran into the kitchen to wrap up the piece of cheesecake she had saved for Burt to eat on his lunch break. "Here you go. Enjoy!"

Burt grinned. "No need to tell me twice." After another salute, he was off with her letter to Liri in one hand and the cheesecake in the other.

Grace stopped at the hall table to pick up the mail—a few ads, the electric bill, and, yes, another letter. She sat on the edge of her chair and grabbed her letter opener. With a flourish that made her feel like Zorro, she flicked the opener under the sealed flap. As she pulled out the stationery, she saw that it was embellished with pink roses along the top, a design similar to one her grandmother would have used. But the signature was a man's. Grace brought the paper closer to her nose and caught the faintest hint of rose petals. The envelope contained an outdated picture of a couple with glasses and graying hair. Their outfits were a monument to the 1970s and a love of polyester.

Dr. Grace,

I was intrigued by your interview on the radio last week. Your story was compelling and made me wonder whether there's any hope for me. I often feel like no one will be able to help me, but here's my story.

I'm eighty-three years old and confined to a wheelchair. Since my wife passed away fifteen years ago, I have spent each miserable day in front of my television, watching the Travel Channel and kicking myself for never taking my wife anywhere. I was always too busy working. I piled up the money—and believe me, we had plenty of it—but I never felt like it was enough. I kept telling myself that we would travel once I retired, but about that time Addie died.

At my wife's funeral, the minister said Addie was now with Jesus and that if I wanted to see her again, I needed to ask Jesus to forgive me so I could go to heaven, too. I thought about what he said, and I closed my eyes and prayed quietly. At first, I felt great, like a lifetime of cares had been washed away. But those good feelings didn't last long. I was soon overwhelmed by anger. I felt worthless and depressed.

For over forty years, my life revolved around work. We moved a lot, but Addie and my son seemed to deal with it all right. After each move, my wife would find a church for her and our son, Matthew, to get involved in. Sure, Matthew would cry for a couple days because he missed his old friends, school, and church, but then he'd straighten up and start acting like a man again.

I gave Matthew everything—a good education, a roof over his head, and a kick in the seat of the pants when he needed it. I even gave him the down payment on his first house. I know I wasn't around much, and I might have been hard on him, but it was for his own good. Like his old dad, he's become quite successful.

Several months after Addie passed, Matt called and told me what a lousy father I had been. That broke my heart. He couldn't have hurt me more if he had stuck a knife in my heart.

Now Matt has completely abandoned me. He doesn't come to see me or even call. He and his wife didn't even have the decency to invite me to my granddaughter's wedding.

Every night I kiss my Addie's picture, and tell her that I love her and that I'll be seeing her soon. But when I hold my son's picture, I feel uncontrollable rage. I can't help but curse him.

My body is failing. The doctors tell me I don't have much time left. I doubt any of my family will come to my funeral. I spent years investing my money to create a trust that would take care of Matt and his family. All that work, and now he doesn't want anything to do with me. I am so angry that I have trouble sleeping. I've contacted my lawyer to draw up a revised will. I plan to leave Matt completely out of it.

The truth is, although my son hurt me, much of what he said was true. It was painful looking in the mirror he held up.

Is there any hope for me?

Victor

There is Hope

Grace set Victor's letter down for a moment and stared thoughtfully out the window. She gazed down the tree-lined street and at the chalk drawings the neighbors' children had made the night before. She turned up her face to the soft breeze passing through. *So much beauty in life, if we only take the time to see it*, she thought. Grace glanced over at the letter and thought of

Victor—imprisoned—but not by his wheelchair. She lifted her pen and began to write.

Dear Victor,

Yes, there is hope for you! First of all, your greatest hope is in knowing that because you accepted Jesus as your Savior, you will go to heaven and see your wife again. Second, even though I wasn't confined to a wheelchair, I have been crippled by anger, resentment, hurt, and unforgiveness, too. As you heard in my radio interview, I have been healed and set free. I'm confident you can be free, too.

I understand at *that moment* your son hurt you deeply and has continued hurting you by withdrawing from having a relationship with you. But Matt hasn't imprisoned you. Your emotions and revenge have done that. I know you are miserable. Let's start here:

When you prayed with the minister at your wife's funeral, Jesus became your Savior. That's wonderful! The Bible says you became a new person. "Therefore, if anyone is in Christ, he is a new creation; old things have passed away; behold, all things have become new" (2 Corinthians 5:17).

You felt the burden of your sin roll away. Now, God wants you to take another positive step by making Jesus your Lord, leader, and boss. Jesus is an excellent boss, and He has perfectly good reasons for telling us what to do or not do. When we are in charge, we mess up our lives and the lives of those we love. Don't you agree?

You could stop right now and tell God that you want Him to be your new boss. You could pray something like this, *Thank you, Jesus, for being my Savior. Now I place You in charge of my life. I want You to be my Lord. I will do what You say.*

Now, as you read the following words from the Bible, what do you think God, your new boss, is asking you to do? The Bible says, "And be kind to one another, tenderhearted, forgiving one another, even as God in Christ forgave you" (Ephesians 4:32). Your new boss is telling you to forgive! Jesus forgave you, and now He wants you to forgive Matt.

You may be thinking, *That's too hard! I can't do it!* But that isn't true. When God is your boss, He gives you everything you need to do what He tells you to do. Where God guides, He provides.

Here's your assignment. I want you to turn off the television for the next several hours and make four lists for me.

Grace continued writing, outlining the four keys to forgiveness and encouraging him to take the steps in each one. She folded the pages and placed them in one of her monogrammed envelopes. Once the envelope was addressed and sealed, she laid her hands on it and began to pray. *Heavenly Father, prepare Victor's heart for this letter. Set him free from his prison of anger, bitterness, and loneliness as he forgives his son. I pray for Your love to fill his heart, in Jesus' name. Amen.*

Grace stamped the letter and stepped onto the front porch to put the letter in the mailbox for Burt to pick up in the morning. As she started down the steps, a car beeped and slowed to a stop. The window rolled down to reveal her beautiful friend, Reverend Shekinah Rhodes, whose photo graced her Freedom Wall. She and Shekinah chatted until a silver SUV pulled up behind her, signaling the end of their conversation. Grace waved and let both cars pass.

Chapter Five

FORGIVING
ABANDONMENT

A s Grace trotted back to her house, she thought about how God was using her forgiveness story to bless others. *Thank you, Jesus!* she prayed. *It's true that the comfort You gave me is being used to comfort others.*

She popped the letter into her mailbox and pulled open her wooden door, still thinking about Shekinah. Grace walked into her office and over to the Freedom Wall. She scanned the faces until she found Shekinah's picture. As she studied the photo, Grace quickly recognized the backdrop as the sculpture garden on the grounds of a museum in town. The sunlight was illuminating Shekinah's beautiful, dark skin. Her hair was arranged in long, thick braids, and she wore a stylish, gray suit and matching hat. *I remember now—she was officiating a wedding on the museum grounds,* Grace thought.

Shekinah was an ordained minister, a gospel singer, and a chaplain for hospice. A couple of years back, her husband, an elder in their church, had an affair with the organist and had walked out on their marriage, leaving her and their twins behind.

Shekinah's feelings had spun out of control for months afterwards. One day, she would be depressed and weepy. The next, she would be filled with anger. The ramifications of her husband's actions were evident in the twins, as well. Their pain and acting out continued to this day. Then there were her financial struggles, her inability to focus at work, and the feelings of shame that caused her to step down from the praise team and drop out of her small group. Every area of her life was negatively affected.

At that low point, she decided to reach out for help, but she wanted a Christian who would give her solid, biblical advice. She had heard the testimony Grace shared at the local Christian Women's Club. Shekinah found Grace after the meeting and exclaimed, "This is exactly the kind of advice I've been looking for!"

They began meeting regularly for coffee. One day, Grace asked Shekinah to bring a legal-sized pad of paper and gave her a four-part assignment. First, she was to make a list of her husband's offenses. Topping her list were unfaithfulness, lying, and abandonment. Shekinah's pen dug deeply into the pad of paper, making several unplanned copies.

Then Grace asked Shekinah to make a second list of the emotions she experienced as a result of *that moment*, both at the time she discovered her husband's affair and the feelings she experienced later.

For the third part of the assignment, Shekinah flipped to a new page so she could write down the domino effect *that moment* caused in other areas of her life. The list took up dozens of lines. Tears smeared the ink across the yellow paper as she relived the painful memories. She chronicled how she could barely function or drag herself out of bed each day to take care of the twins and go to work.

Shekinah thumbed through her smudged pages and was hit by a revelation. "Sister Grace," Shekinah said, "when you told me I was a prisoner to my unforgiveness, I thought you were crazy, but creating these lists shows me you were right. So much of my suffering has been because I haven't forgiven him," she confessed. "He didn't create the domino effect. I did!"

Grace gave a sympathetic nod and asked her to make a fourth list—one for the negative ways she had reacted to *that moment*. Shekinah's pen no longer scratched through several layers of paper as before. Instead, the ink was so light that it was a bit difficult to read. God opened Shekinah's eyes to her own sinfulness. She hadn't committed adultery, but she had sinned with her words and actions, including the refusal to forgive.

"Until today I could only see my husband's sin," Shekinah said. "Now I realize how much I need forgiveness, too. What do I do with these four lists?"

"God has given you the four keys to set you free," said Grace. "Let's use them."

Grace walked her through using the first key: forgiving the offenses on her first list. Then they used the second key: forgiving her husband for all of the different emotions caused by the offense.

Shekinah prayed, *I choose to forgive my husband for the feelings that I experienced because of what he did—anger, bitterness, worthlessness…* On and on her words flowed, until she closed her prayer with the words, *The blood of Jesus covers those feelings.*

With Grace's help, Shekinah used the third and fourth keys to forgive her husband for all the ways the offense affected other areas of her life and to ask for forgiveness for her own sinful reactions to it. The forgiveness prayers that flowed from the coffee shop that morning didn't change the fact that her husband had an affair or that the twins' father wasn't around. It didn't change the fact that Shekinah was struggling financially as a single mother, but they did change her heart. She walked out of her prison—free at last.

Shekinah's freedom enabled her to return to being a wonderful mother and providing for her girls' needs—physically, educationally, emotionally, and spiritually. The twins, Trinity and D'Zion, were growing up to be lovely young ladies, so talented, smart, and sweet. Shekinah made sure they ate dinner together each evening and shared devotions at bedtime. They loved harmonizing their voices in praise songs from church, reading, acting out stories from their *Action Bible*, and talking about their day. They prayed together and even enjoyed the occasional pillow fight.

The love that flowed from her life was a testimony to the whole community and opened doors for her to teach and sing throughout the area. Shekinah's family was living out the truth in Proverbs 4:18, which says, "But the path of the just is like the shining sun, That shines ever brighter unto the perfect day."

Chapter Six

FALSE VS. TRUE FORGIVENESS

◡

The morning was beautiful and cool—too beautiful to be inside. Grace doctored her morning coffee and headed onto the front porch with her mail. She curled up on the faded floral cushion of the wicker rocker. She breathed in deeply, enjoying the breeze, the morning sun, and the aroma of fresh-cut grass still moist from the morning dew.

She picked up an envelope from the stack. The outside of this one seemed familiar to her. She looked at the return address and saw that it was from Victor. As she opened the letter and began to read, she wondered how things were going with his son.

> Dr. Grace,
>
> I finished the four lists you told me to write. They were so long that I just about used up all of Addie's stationery. It's going to be very difficult to forget the many ways Matt has hurt me. This assignment made me feel very angry. I don't see how it's supposed to help. I've only opened a can of worms. I feel worse than I did before. What do I do with these lists?
>
> Victor
>
> P.S. This is a short letter because my hand is tired.

It had only been a little more than a week since Grace had read Victor's first letter. She was encouraged that he had taken these steps already. She wrote back:

Dear Victor,

I know it's hard to relive hurtful situations, but you've already taken a huge step toward being set free.

Let me explain a couple of essential points concerning forgiveness. There is false forgiveness. When people think they have forgiven because they are trying to forget about an offense (which is quite impossible), or when they are excusing the offense or pretending it didn't matter, it is false forgiveness. False forgiveness doesn't set people free. It may bury the hurt, but it won't be long before it starts crawling out again.

There is also incomplete forgiveness. People forgive one part of the offense, but not the whole thing. Therefore, they continue to be imprisoned by their emotions, the ramifications, and their sinful reactions.

True and complete forgiveness is choosing to accept the blood of Jesus as the full payment for:

- what the offender did at *that moment,*
- how you felt (the emotions) as a result of *that moment,*
- how *that moment* has affected other areas of your life, and
- your sinful reactions toward the offender, God, yourself, and others.

God didn't forgive your sins by pretending you didn't do anything wrong, trying to forget that you sinned, or letting time pass. Someone had to pay the penalty for those sins. Jesus paid that penalty, and because He forgave you, you are commanded and able to forgive others.

Grace continued writing, explaining how to use the four keys of forgiveness, then sealed the letter. She placed her hands on the envelope and prayed aloud. *Heavenly Father, help Victor use the keys explained in this letter to forgive his son. Touch his heart and set him free. In Jesus' name.*

When Grace looked up at the clock, she shook her head in amazement. *Time flies when you're having fun,* she thought. *Yes, fun!* Her friends often asked if it bothered her to listen to people's sad stories. Her answer was always the same: *It's sad to hear the many ways people have been hurt by others, but when they write to me, I get excited because I know they're going to be healed and set free.*

Grace put a stamp on Victor's letter and set it on the hall table by the door, thinking, *I'll put it in the mailbox tomorrow morning. I need to prepare for my talk at Bible study tonight.*

Several Hours Later

That evening, after everyone was seated—some on couches, some on chairs, some cross-legged on the floor—the worship leader closed his eyes and began strumming his guitar. As each praise song unfolded, voices blended to create a sweet chorus. After he finished his set of songs, the leader nodded to Grace to begin her message for the evening. She opened her Bible to where she had filled three pages of notes and cleared her throat.

"I was asked to share tonight on the freedom found through forgiveness, which is actually my favorite subject to talk about." She gave everyone a broad smile. Grace's unpretentious manner put the group at ease and captured their full attention. "The reason I love to speak on forgiveness is because when I forgave the people who hurt me, it changed my life and set me free.

"I was listening to the Christian radio station during my walk today when the song 'Forgiveness' by Matthew West came on. I'd like to read the lyrics to you."

Grace began reading the first stanza.

It's the hardest thing to give away
And the last thing on your mind today
It always goes to those who don't deserve
It's the opposite of how you feel
When the pain they caused is just too real
Takes everything you have to say the word—
Forgiveness!

Grace hadn't noticed that the guitarist had picked up his instrument until he began to softly pick out the chords to the song and accompany her.

It flies in the face of all your pride
It moves away the mad inside

It's always anger's own worst enemy
Even when the jury and the judge
Say you've got a right to hold a grudge
It's the whisper in your ear saying, 'Set it free'
Forgiveness!

The guitar strings vibrated louder as several in the group joined in on the chorus.

Show me how to love the unlovable
Show me how to reach the unreachable
Help me now to do the impossible—
Forgiveness!

As more and more of the members chimed in, Grace's voice moved from reading to singing the words.

It'll clear the bitterness away
It can even set a prisoner free
There is no end to what its power can do
So let it go and be amazed by what you see through eyes of grace
The prisoner that it really frees is you—
Forgiveness!

The final word, "forgiveness," hung in the air, and the guitarist allowed the last chord to vibrate until it faded away.

"The prisoner that forgiveness really frees is you," Grace said quietly. The listeners seemed to lean in closer to hear her. Grace thought of her own time in the prison of unforgiveness and shuddered.

"I, too, was a prisoner, freed by forgiveness."

She took a breath, and composed herself. No matter how many times she told this story, it still took a lot out of her.

"When I was seven years old, I was molested by an adult member of our church." Grace's statement sent a jolt through the room. That was the effect Grace had expected. She knew there was a big difference between singing a song about forgiveness and actually walking it out.

"I have a right to hold a grudge. Right?" She looked around for someone to reply, but everyone was quiet, still taken aback by her openness. Before Grace looked down at her notes, she noticed a girl in the corner holding back some tears. *I need to talk with her after the study,* she thought.

"By the world's standards, I had the right to refuse to forgive him, but that didn't do me any good. Unforgiveness wasn't the prescription for healing my wounds. It was a recipe for poisoning my life.

"My thinking became contaminated—scary dreams each night, disgusting mental pictures, and awful thoughts about myself and life. I rejected anyone who claimed to be a Christian. My emotions were completely out of control, like riding a bobsled down Mount Everest." Grace counted on her fingers as she listed the emotions. "Fear, shame, depression, anxiety, anger, just to name a few.

"You can probably imagine that being abused had an awful effect on my physical body, too. It made any kind of physical affection intolerable. I didn't want anyone to touch me, not even my father."

Grace's eyes slowly moved around the room, gauging the impact of her testimony. Those who found her story too intense were looking down at their Bibles or fiddling with their phones. Others were hanging on every word. She took special note of the girl in the corner, thinking, *She knows exactly what I'm talking about.*

Grace brushed a wisp of dark brown hair away from her face and continued, "Every area of my life was ripped apart, all because of the evil someone chose to commit against me. I was a mess, and if God hadn't set me free, the dominoes would still be falling.

"How many of you are familiar with the story of Joseph in the book of Genesis?"

Grace quickly glanced around at the hands raised and saw that a couple of new girls still had their hands in their laps. "Let me recap the story because it is a remarkable account of forgiving those who have hurt you.

"Joseph was the eleventh son in his family. His brothers were jealous of him because he was their father's favorite. In fact, Joseph's brothers hated him so much that they sold him into slavery. He was taken into Egypt, far from his home, his father, and his country. At one point, he was falsely accused of attacking a rich man's wife and thrown into prison.

"To make a long story short, God was with Joseph through all of his many trials. In fact, once he was freed from prison, God placed him second in command to Pharaoh because Joseph had warned the ruler of a terrible famine to come. When the famine arrived as Joseph predicted, people from many countries came to Egypt to buy grain, including Joseph's brothers." Grace raised her eyebrows to emphasize the point.

"When Joseph's brothers stood before him to request grain, Joseph recognized them, but they didn't recognize him. It had been over ten years since they had seen him, and they probably figured he was dead by then.

"Joseph said to his brothers, 'I am Joseph!' Knowing they had treated him so viciously, they were afraid for their lives. Then Joseph said, 'Come here. I am your brother, the one you sold! What you meant for evil God has used for good. He has put me here to save you and keep our family from starving.'

"Joseph had been terribly mistreated by his brothers, just like I had been terribly mistreated by a 'brother.'" Grace wiggled her fingers like imaginary quotation marks. "Joseph learned that God can turn the evil things others do to us into something good. In fact, Romans 8:28 says, 'And we know that all things work together for good to those who love God, to those who are the called according to His purpose.'

"That's exactly what God has done for me. He has taken the evil that was done to me and miraculously worked it together for my good. He has a destiny and purpose for my life, which is explained in the very next verse: 'For whom He foreknew, He also predestined to be conformed to the image of His Son, that He might be the firstborn among many brethren' (Romans 8:29).

"God is molding me—and you," Grace said as she looked at a couple of the listeners, "into the image of His Son so that when people look at us, they see Jesus—His love, His forgiveness, His acceptance, His mercy.

"Jesus understands pain, betrayal, and rejection. He's been there. Isaiah 53:3 talks about the treatment He received. It says, 'He is despised and rejected by men, A Man of sorrows and acquainted with grief. And we hid, as it were, our faces from Him; He was despised, and we did not esteem Him.'

"After experiencing the worst abuse that any of us can imagine, Jesus said, 'Father, forgive them.' I'm glad God is using everything I have gone through—the good, the bad, and the ugly—to conform me into the kind of person He wants me to be. Are you glad He's doing that for you, too? It gives incredible value to everything we go through. God will use it all to make us more like Jesus and let it minister to others." Grace's heart warmed when she saw people nodding in agreement.

"Do you want to forgive those who have hurt you instead of holding on to your pain? If so, I have a twenty-one-day forgiveness challenge that will walk you through the process of forgiving others." Grace reached into her tote bag and pulled out a stack of booklets. She walked over and handed them to the young lady in the corner and asked, "Would you please pass these around to everyone?"

The young lady looked startled, as if surprised that anyone had noticed her. She took a booklet and handed the rest to the couple next to her. "I hope you will take the challenge," Grace continued. "Forgiveness set me free, and God has turned to good what the enemy meant for evil."

Grace sat down and leaned back in her chair. She tucked her notes back into her Bible and closed it, signaling the end of the lesson.

The worship leader thanked Grace for being transparent about her own life and led in a closing prayer. Some in the group made their way over to thank Grace and let her know they would take the challenge. She told them to send her their picture and story, and she would add them to her Freedom Wall.

The girl in the corner hung back until Grace was available, and then she walked over. She hesitated, and Grace smiled and said, "I was hoping I could talk with you before you left." The girl's eyes filled with tears at the compassion in Grace's voice. She thought, *Once again, Lord, You are working together all the things I've gone through for good.*

Chapter Seven

DO I NEED TO FORGIVE GOD?

The next morning, Grace sat on her front porch, drinking a cup of coffee. Her box of monogrammed stationery, Bible, and pen were arranged on the small table beside her. She held her coffee mug in both hands against her chin, deep in thought, and then suddenly set the mug down. She reached for her pen and began writing to the young lady she'd met the night before, the one who had sat silently in the corner.

Grace wasn't aware that hours had passed until Burt came bounding up the front steps. She jerked back in her seat. "Oh my gosh! You startled me," she said.

"Sorry, Dr. Grace. I should whistle while I work so people can hear me comin'." Burt smiled and nodded toward the stack of stationery on her lap. "Writing another letter, I see."

"Yes, I met a young woman at Bible study last night." Grace stacked the seven pages of her letter neatly, then tried to stand. She'd been sitting all morning and her legs had fallen asleep. She groaned as needles seemed to poke up and down her calves. "I made a toffee truffle cheesecake for the group last night, and I saved you the best piece. I'll go get it—if I can move my legs." She hobbled slightly as she went down the hall to the kitchen.

When Grace stepped back onto the porch, Burt grinned and handed her the clean Tupperware container from last time. Grace laughed. "I don't always get those back." She examined it and exclaimed, "Wow! You even cleaned it. You're a good egg."

"That's why I brought it back. I didn't want you to beat me."

"That was fowl!" Grace smirked.

Burt was clearly ready to shoot back. "You crack me up, Dr. Grace!"

"Well, what can you expect? It's Fry-day Get it? Fry-day!" She tried to stifle a laugh, but it came out anyway.

"Are you cackling? I think you're cackling," he joked.

Grace laughed a little louder. "Stop poaching all of my best yolks."

"Just trying to keep your sunny side up. Okay, that's my last one so don't keep egging me on. Oops!" Burt covered his mouth with his hand and feigned a shocked look.

Through the laughs, Grace hiccupped, "I don't want to hear another peep out of you." Burt and Grace erupted into laughter, causing an older lady walking down the sidewalk to give them a quizzical look. Once the laughter died down, Grace grew thoughtful. "It's so good to have someone to laugh at corny puns with."

Burt nodded. "I have you to thank for that—for being able to laugh again."

Grace nodded knowingly. She stayed quiet, leaving him space to talk, if he wanted.

"After Chris died, I didn't think I'd ever laugh again," Burt continued. "I was so angry with God. If it weren't for you, I don't think I would have realized that I didn't need to forgive God for taking my son. God didn't do anything wrong. Now that I realize that, I can say that God is good all the time."

Grace put her hand on Burt's. "You're right. We may never know why certain things happen to us or to those we love, but we can know God's love, healing, and comfort through it."

He nodded. "I'm sure glad He took all that anger away. I remember sitting right here on your porch and forgiving poor old Mr. Robinson. I know he didn't mean to do it. He never even saw Chris run out in front of his car."

Grace reflected back to that evening, how tears had streamed down both of their cheeks. She sent up a silent prayer: *Thank you, Jesus, for coming to bring life and defeat the works of the enemy. You're so good.*

"You helped me realize I didn't need to forgive God," Burt said. "There was nothing to forgive. Instead, I found myself asking God for forgiveness for being angry that He wasn't doing things my way."

Grace nodded in agreement, "Our Heavenly Father understands how it feels to lose a son." She remembered God's comfort and love being almost tangible when they had prayed together on the porch.

As Grace was talking, a gold luxury SUV pulled up in front of the house. On the passenger door was a magnetic sign that read Reynolds Real Estate. A tall blonde woman in a skirted suit slid out and popped the back open. She reached in and lifted out a For Sale sign. Her heels made a soft clicking noise as she walked up the sidewalk toward Grace, holding the sign in perfectly manicured hands.

Grace almost dove off of the porch. "Wait a minute—you must be making a mistake. This house is not for sale."

The blonde shot Grace a phony smile. "Actually, it is."

Burt looked back and forth between the two women.

Grace gasped. "But I've been renting this house for eight years. The owners never told me they wanted to sell."

"Take it up with them. If you'd like to make an offer, I'm all ears." With an unfeminine heave, she plunged the spikes into the grass.

Grace stood with her mouth open as the agent flicked her hair over her shoulder and strode to her chariot. When the SUV sped away, the tires churned through a pile of dry leaves that had been collecting along the curb.

"I can't believe it," Grace moaned. "I just can't believe the Brannons are selling my house."

Burt rested his hand on her shoulder. "I'm sorry. Maybe God has something better for you."

Ooh, I don't feel like hearing that right now, she thought.

When Burt left to finish his mail delivery for the day, Grace was still standing by the sign in the grass. She had lived in the house for years, and with the Brannons' encouragement, she had made it her own. She had planted flower gardens, renovated one of the bedrooms into an office, and trimmed out the exterior to match her unique tastes. It had become her dream home. There wasn't another one like it in Midland.

I can't believe the Brannons would pull the rug out from under me like that, she thought morosely. *Just the other day, they reassured me that they weren't planning to sell. What total posers they are for sending their real estate agent instead of telling me themselves.*

Then anger was replaced by fear. *Oh my gosh! Did I do something wrong? I've paid my rent each month on time—well, mostly. Is this because I was late a few times? What am I going to do? I love this house.*

That Night

Grace dreamed of sleeping on a narrow prison cot, the shadow from the steel bars striping the floor of her cell. That night she heard heavy footsteps coming down the hallway. She saw that word again, *basanizo*—torment—etched into the wall. After struggling to wake up, she found herself in her own bed. She rolled out onto her knees and cried out, *God, I've fallen back into the prison of unforgiveness. I went to bed angry, and the enemy has gotten a foothold.*

Grace remained in the place of prayer, using each of the keys of forgiveness. She forgave the Brannons for putting the house up for sale without notifying her. She forgave the real estate agent for her rudeness. She forgave them all for the fear and anguish this had caused her. She closed the prayer by repenting for making judgments of the Brannons and the agent.

Grace's dark hair fanned out on her white cotton sheets. Tears rolled over her cheeks, and she dried them on her pajama sleeve as she prayed. *Lord, You are good all the time. I don't understand why this is happening, but I put my trust in You. I let go of my anger, bitterness, and unforgiveness. Thank you for the blood of Jesus covering my sins.* A soft glow filled the room, and peace settled on Grace like the morning dew.

Chapter Eight

DO I NEED TO FORGIVE MYSELF?

The sun was barely up, but Grace couldn't tell. It was raining, so there would be no sitting on the porch today. She flipped on her computer and wandered into the kitchen to decide about breakfast. When she returned, steaming oatmeal in hand, she was intrigued by an email with a familiar last name—Paine. But it wasn't from Liri; it was from her husband, Cliff.

> From: cliff@cliffordpaine.me
> Sent: Monday, February 23, 2015 8:38 PM
> To: Dr. Grace
> Subject: Question
>
> Good evening, Dr. Grace,
>
> Yesterday, I found some letters you wrote to my wife, Liri. I was probably wrong for reading them, but I was looking for answers to why Liri's been acting so different lately. She's been happier than she has been in years. Even though she's never liked my job much, every day for the last week, she's left me notes around the house, thanking me for providing for the family and for working hard. She used to do things like that years ago, but she hasn't for a long time.
>
> At first, I thought she was buttering me up so she could divorce me, but I'm starting to wonder if she's for real. I see her reading her Bible and praying for our little girl, Abigail. She even went to church on Sunday.

You'd think these changes would make me happy, but they are making me mad. She's so nice that I feel guilty for what I've done to her—talking her into having sex while we were dating, demanding she have an abortion, criticizing her. I could go on and on.

I want our marriage to work, but I don't know how to change. I've never told anyone about this, but when I was young, my best friend in middle school dared me to look at some porn in his parents' garage. I've been addicted ever since. Liri had been wondering why I was staying up so late and why our sexual relationship had changed. When she found out why, it about killed her.

Part of me blamed my failing marriage on my friend because he got me started. In your letters, you explained how to forgive, and I used those keys to forgive him. I believe God used them to set me free from pornography, but I don't think I can ever forgive myself for what I have done to Liri and our unborn child.

How do I forgive myself?

Cliff Paine

Grace closed her eyes briefly and said a silent prayer. Then she began to type.

Good morning, Cliff!

Thank you for your email. I'm so glad you used the keys of forgiveness to forgive your friend. You will experience greater and greater freedom as you read the Bible and focus on God, who is calling you to renew your mind.

Here's what Philippians 4:8 says: "Finally, brethren, whatever things are true, whatever things are noble, whatever things are just, whatever things are pure, whatever things are lovely, whatever things are of good report, if there is any virtue and if there is anything praiseworthy—meditate on these things."

To decide if your thoughts fit that Scripture or not, I like to say, "If it doesn't believe the best, it doesn't pass the test."

You asked how to forgive yourself. I understand you have a great deal of shame and regret for the pain you've caused, but the only one who is worthy to judge you is God, and He sent Jesus to pay for your sins. Here's what James 4:12 says: "There is one Lawgiver, who is able to save and to destroy. Who are you to judge another?"

That verse says God sets the standards and judges according to those standards. He gives salvation or punishment—we don't. That includes punishing ourselves. When we condemn ourselves, we are taking God's role. If we ask God to forgive our sins, Jesus' blood covers those sins. Hebrews 9:22b says, "And without shedding of blood there is no remission [of sin]." A person would have to live a perfect life and shed perfect innocent blood in order to have his own sins forgiven. None of us can do that—but Jesus did. His blood covers all of our sins perfectly. You can't do that for yourself. Your sins of immorality, lust, abortion, pornography—they have all been forgiven.

Right now, you could pray the following prayer and be set free from guilt and condemnation:

Heavenly Father, I confess I've been judging myself and holding myself guilty. I repent of judging myself and competing with You. You are God, and I am not. Thank you for forgiving all of my sins and failures. This day, I receive Your total forgiveness. In Jesus' name. Amen.

Grace paused for a moment, thinking back to her exchanges with Liri. Then she began to write again.

I know Liri wants the marriage to work, too, Cliff. Your assignment is to think about how you have hurt Liri, then go to her and ask her to forgive you.

You could say something like this: "Liri, I was wrong for pressuring you to break your purity vow and have sex before we married. Please forgive me. I also ask your forgiveness for coercing you into having an abortion. I was so wrong. Would you please forgive me?"

You can take it from here, Cliff. Please let me know how it goes.

Blessings,

Dr. Grace

By the way, please send me your picture. I have a special wall that has the pictures of everyone who has been set free from guilt. I'd love to remember you as one of those people.

Chapter Nine

BREAKING FREE
OF CONTROL

As Grace lay awake in bed that night, her mind drifted over the past several weeks. So much had happened, with Bible study, Liri and Cliff, Shekinah, Burt, and Victor and his son.

Her mind rested a moment on Victor. What had she written about in her last letter? He had written out the four lists, and she had told him how to use those lists to forgive. But something was nagging at her, something she had forgotten to say.

She thought of Victor's son, and suddenly she sat upright in her dark bedroom. At that moment, she knew just what Victor still needed to hear from her. *How the Holy Spirit moves*, she thought.

She went to her office, turned on her desk lamp, and in the quiet stillness wrote one more letter to Victor.

Dear Victor,

In your last letter, you asked me to help you understand why Matthew turned against you and what you could do to restore your relationship with him.

First, we should talk about the difference between human authority, like a parent over a child, and God's authority over us. God's authority is perfect. Human authority is not. Take a look at this diagram:

Try to remember how you were treated by nearly everyone in a position of authority. They were sure to let you know who was the boss (authority), right? You might have been told there would be consequences if you failed to comply (accountability). If you fell in line with those rules, you might have gotten some recognition (affirmation). If you were careful, you might even have started feeling like you were approved (acceptance). That's the way of the world—authority first, accountability second, affirmation third, and (if you make it) acceptance last.

That's the way parents, teachers, bosses, or spouses get someone to do what they want them to do. It is control. Even if it's well-meaning, it's still control. Acceptance is based on performance. "You do what I want you to do, and I'll accept you." Like many concepts in this world, it's the wrong way around. It's upside-down, but it's hard to blame people for doing it. In most cases, it's the only approach they've ever known.

Our mistake is in thinking the Lord treats us the same way. "These things you have done, and I kept silent; You thought that I was altogether like you" (Psalm 50:21a). God comes at it from the other direction: not control, but love. He offers acceptance and affirmation first because His acceptance is based on the finished work of Christ and not on our performance.

How do people react when they are being controlled? As you might expect, they rebel. Is it possible that is what is happening with

Matt? Is it possible that your love and acceptance for him were conditional, based on his performance? Were you controlling with him? Maybe you weren't trying to be, but what does his reaction tell you?

Everywhere you look, people are crying out to be accepted. That includes Matt. I know you love him. What can you do to demonstrate your love and acceptance, Victor? Ask God to show you three ways you can reach out to Matt and his family; then do them.

Blessings,

Dr. Grace

Chapter Ten

LIFE REIGNS
OVER DEATH

⌒

A month later, Grace quickly crossed the front porch in her robe and slippers to pick up the paper hidden beneath the colorful litter of fall leaves. She gave it a shake and hurried back inside.

She fixed herself a sliver of her latest creation—pumpkin pecan cheesecake. After cutting off the very tip with the edge of her fork, she popped it into her mouth. *Mmm!* she thought, *my favorite kind of breakfast.*

Between bites of cheesecake and sips of strong coffee, Grace skimmed through the paper. She didn't usually read the obituaries, but today her eye caught a familiar name: Victor Vallet. *Oh my gosh, Lord!* She noted the graveside service was to be held at 10 a.m. on Saturday at Resthaven Memorial Park. She reached for her iPad and quickly ordered flowers to be sent.

She prayed, *Lord, I don't know how much of what I shared with Victor he applied, but Your Word does not return void. It always accomplishes much. Thank you for the little bit of time You allowed for me to get to know him. Despite all that has happened, I hope his family goes to the funeral to pay their respects.*

Saying Goodbye

That Saturday morning, Grace dressed in her warm black wool suit and slipped on her low-heeled boots. It was a little chilly, but the sun was shining. *I'm glad for that, Lord. It's less dreary when the sky is blue.*

At 10 a.m., Grace pulled into the graveyard on the north side of town and headed toward the small green tent about one hundred feet away. Seats had been set up under the tent, and beside them was a mound of dirt covered with a blanket of artificial grass.

As she slipped under the canvas tent and lay her coat over a folding chair, Grace counted only a handful of people. The minister rose and began singing a soulful rendition of "Amazing Grace." Grace couldn't help but smile. It was Shekinah. She must have met Victor at hospice.

Shekinah's voice rose. "When we've been there ten thousand years, bright shining as the sun…" The words stirred Grace's heart as she thought about Victor now being in heaven with his wife and his Lord and Savior, Jesus.

Shekinah ended the song with a gospel flair that would have satisfied the most ardent music lover, then began to read the same obituary Grace had read in the paper.

> Victor Vallet was born in Midland, Texas, to Art and Victoria Lamb Vallet on June 14, 1930. He attended Midland High School and graduated in 1948. As Cadet Second Lieutenant of the Infantry regiment, he earned a business degree from Texas A&M in College Station, Texas. He worked forty-plus years in the transportation and material moving business, which took the family to almost every state in the Midwest.
>
> Victor is preceded in death by his parents; three brothers, Gregory, Dennis, and Douglas Vallet; and his wife, Adeline.
>
> Victor is survived by his son, Matthew Vallet of Midland, and his granddaughter, Addie.

Shekinah paused and met Grace's eyes before beginning her message.

"I met Victor three months ago through hospice. Each day I visited him, Victor would show me the picture of his wife. We would talk about her and the places they had lived. He missed her terribly and was looking forward to being reunited with her in heaven. He also talked a lot about his son, Matt, and how proud he was of him. Victor will be missed, but we know that he made peace with God. He is now in the presence of his Lord, Jesus. Would you like to say a few words, Matt?"

Matt slowly stood and moved up in front of the coffin, which was waiting to be lowered into the earth. "I'd like to say my dad and I had a great relationship through the years, but that wouldn't be true. We didn't talk much.

He wasn't around when I was growing up, since he was always working. I thought I didn't need a dad for most of my life.

"But in the past few weeks, something changed. He started calling just to ask how we were doing and if we needed anything. He even wrote a couple of letters telling me how proud he was of me." Matt's voice broke slightly.

"The week before he died, he invited me to meet him at his favorite barbecue place. Over a pound of brisket, he asked me to forgive him for lots of things, including not being a good father, for being critical, for being controlling, and for hanging up on us—everything. Our relationship had been dead for so many years, but right then, it came back to life.

"I didn't know it, but dad had sought help from a Christian counselor. I can't remember when he ever asked for help from anyone, let alone a Christian. But as I was going through his papers the other day, I found the letters the counselor had sent him—a letter on how to make Jesus your Lord, a letter on how to forgive, and a letter on how to be a good dad.

"I had been deeply hurt by my father, and I had vowed to never be like him. But I know that I've made mistakes as a father, too.

"As I read through those letters, I took a long, hard look at my own life. My dad finally got it right. He did something I truly admire. He humbly asked for my forgiveness. Today I want to be like him."

Matt looked over at his daughter, who was seated in the front row and had tears streaming down her face. "Addie, will you please forgive me for not being a good dad, for being so controlling and authoritative? I see how wrong I've been, honey." Tears welled up in his eyes.

Addie rushed to her father's side and said, "Daddy, of course, I forgive you. Thank you for asking. I love you!"

Shekinah pulled out a hankie from her jacket and handed it to Matt. She placed her hands on Matt and Addie, and began to pray:

Heavenly Father, thank you for Your forgiveness for our failures and sins. Thank you for healing and restoring this family. Wash away the brokenness of the past. Let this be the beginning of a new day. Thank you for Victor's life ending well. This is his legacy—forgiveness.

The family filed past the coffin, each one pausing to say goodbye. Grace moved forward to do the same. *Victor, you'd be so happy to see what just hap-*

pened. This was like no other funeral I've ever seen. God set you free, and you helped your son and granddaughter to be free, too, Grace thought.

Grace gave her condolences to the family, and Shekinah gave Grace a knowing hug.

As she turned to leave, a man who had been sitting behind the family introduced himself as Victor's attorney and handed her an envelope. Grace brought the envelope to her nose. *Yes, there's the smell of roses,* she thought. *How funny!* She smiled and stepped outside of the tent to open the letter.

Dear Dr. Grace,

I finished my last assignment of meeting with Matt to ask for his forgiveness. God helped me come up with a list of things I had said and done to hurt him over the years. I was surprised it was so long.

I can't thank you enough for your encouragement to forgive and seek forgiveness of Matt, but I'm going to try. The man who gave you this letter is my lawyer. Remember I told you I was going to write Matt out of my will? Well, I didn't do that, but I did make some other changes. I wrote you into it.

My lawyer has the deed to your house, which I purchased for you when it came up for sale. I've also arranged for you to receive a monthly allowance so you can cut back on your hours at work and expand your ministry to poor old prisoners like I used to be.

See you in heaven,

Victor

Grace's knees buckled under her. She reached out to steady herself, then found a seat and sat down. She inhaled deeply and said out loud: *Thank you, Jesus!* She was struck by the perfection of God's plan. He had known from the beginning that Victor would need her and that she would need Victor. She looked over at Matt and his daughter, who were sitting next to each other. Addie was crying, and Matt had his arm around her. Grace thought, *God is good, all the time.*

CONCLUSION

As you reach the end of this book, I pray that you will be more than just a reader. I pray that you will take action on what you have learned in these pages. James 1:22 says, "But be doers of the word, and not hearers only, deceiving yourselves." Be like the people in this book—take a step of faith. Take the 21-Day Forgiveness Challenge and experience transformation and freedom in your own life.

Keep in mind that forgiveness isn't just a one-time event—it's a lifestyle. Keep this book close and refer to it the next time someone hurts you. Matthew 18:21–22 says, "Then Peter came to Him and said, 'Lord, how often shall my brother sin against me, and I forgive him? Up to seven times?' Jesus said to him, 'I do not say to you, up to seven times, but up to seventy times seven.'" We are to forgive as often as it takes.

Don't keep the keys to freedom to yourself, either. Consider passing one of these books through the bars to a friend or someone you know who is still in the prison of unforgiveness.

Freedom awaits!

APPENDIX

21-DAY FORGIVENESS CHALLENGE

*D*o you have a moment in your life that is *that moment* for you? A time when your life was torn apart by someone else? Do you have trouble being able to forgive because the hurt was so deep? If so, I invite you to be set free from your prison of unforgiveness.

Maybe you're having trouble narrowing it down to one *moment* because the offense went on for years. Choose one specific incident to help you start the healing process, but remember that when someone hurts you with the same repeated offense over and over again, we must also choose to keep on forgiving again and again.

"Then Peter came to Him and said, 'Lord, how often shall my brother sin against me, and I forgive him? Up to seven times?' Jesus said to him, 'I do not say to you, up to seven times, but up to seventy times seven'" (Matthew 18:21–22).

When we refuse to forgive, whether it's something that occurred in a single *moment* or over a lifetime of *moments*, we become locked away in solitude. We will only be free when we accept the freedom that God extends to us through the four keys of forgiveness.

Take this 21-Day Forgiveness Challenge. It walks you step-by-step down the path to granting true and complete forgiveness.

DAY 1

ave you asked Jesus to forgive your sins and come into your life? If so, describe that event. If not, would you like Jesus to be your Savior, the forgiver of your sins? You could pray something like this:

Dear Jesus, I believe in You. I believe that You are the Son of God and You died for my sins. I believe God has raised You from the dead and that You are Lord of all creation. Please forgive me for all my sins. Cleanse my heart with Your precious blood. I trust You now, as my Lord and Savior. Thank you, Lord! In Your name I pray. Amen!

If you just prayed for Jesus to come into your heart, how would you describe the experience? You may or may not feel any different. The important thing is knowing that you have become a child of God and have eternal life.

_____

_____

_____

_____

_____

_____

_____

_____

_____

_____

_____

DAY 2

*J*esus wants to be your Savior and your Lord, the leader and boss of your life. Ask Him to be your Lord by praying something like the following:

Jesus, I want You to take charge of my life. I surrender my will to You. Please instruct, direct, and correct me. I will obey what You tell me to do. Amen.

Now spend time asking your leader (boss) for guidance, instruction, and direction. Describe what He is revealing to you.

_____

_____

_____

_____

_____

_____

_____

_____

_____

_____

_____

_____

_____

_____

_____

DAY 3

"Bearing with one another, and forgiving one another, if anyone has a complaint against another; even as Christ forgave you, so you also must do" (Colossians 3:13).

In this Scripture, what do you think the Lord (your leader) is telling you, specifically, to do? Is there a person who comes to mind when you read it? If so, who? Write down what God is telling you to do.

_____

_____

_____

_____

_____

_____

_____

_____

_____

_____

_____

_____

_____

_____

_____

DAY 4

ave you thought you forgave someone, only to realize later that it was either false forgiveness or incomplete forgiveness?

False forgiveness is simply:
- trying to forget about *that moment*
- letting time pass after *that moment*
- excusing or disregarding the wrong another person has done against you
- pretending *that moment* did not matter

True and complete forgiveness is choosing to accept the blood of Jesus as the full payment for:
- what your offender did at *that moment*
- how you felt as a result of *that moment*
- how *that moment* has affected other areas of your life
- your sinful reactions to *that moment*

Explain what false forgiveness or incomplete forgiveness has looked like in your life.

_____

_____

_____

_____

_____

_____

_____

_____

DAY 5

*W*rite about what *that moment* has been for you. Explain the offense: who, what, when, where, and how it happened.

_____

_____

_____

_____

_____

_____

_____

_____

_____

_____

_____

_____

_____

_____

_____

_____

_____

_____

_____

DAY 6

 ~

*L*ist the emotions or painful feelings you experienced as a result of *that moment*. (To help you think through the full range of emotions you might have experienced, see the List of Feelings in the Appendix.) What were your feelings then, later, and now?

_____

_____

_____

_____

_____

_____

_____

_____

_____

_____

_____

_____

_____

_____

_____

_____

_____

DAY 7

*I*f you don't forgive the person or people who have hurt you, the poison of *that moment* will taint every area of your life. What areas of your life (relationships, thoughts, finances, marriage, parenting, job, dreams, goals, fellowship with God, etc.) have been affected?

_____

_____

_____

_____

_____

_____

_____

_____

_____

_____

_____

_____

_____

_____

_____

_____

_____

DAY 8

When people sinned against Jesus at *that moment*, He chose to forgive His offenders, saying, "Father, forgive them, for they do not know what they do" (Luke 23:34a). In *that moment* in your life, did you respond like Jesus or did you react sinfully? (For example: speak unkind words or act in a hurtful manner to your offender? It could also include gossiping, slandering, rejecting, and judging your offender.)

List your sinful thoughts and actions.

_____

_____

_____

_____

_____

_____

_____

_____

_____

_____

_____

_____

_____

_____

_____

_____

DAY 9

⁓

God commands us to forgive when we are hurt and offended, not to condemn or seek revenge. How does the following verse line up with the choices you have made? "[Jesus] who, when He was reviled, did not revile in return; when He suffered, He did not threaten, but committed Himself to Him who judges righteously" (1 Peter 2:23).

_____

_____

_____

_____

_____

_____

_____

_____

_____

_____

_____

_____

_____

_____

_____

DAY 10

"There is one Lawgiver, who is able to save and to destroy. Who are you to judge another?" (James 4:12). In what ways have you been sitting as the judge and condemning (or seeking to destroy) those who have wronged you? Have you been refusing to forgive because they should pay for their wrongs?

_____

_____

_____

_____

_____

_____

_____

_____

_____

_____

_____

_____

_____

_____

_____

_____

DAY 11

$\mathcal{R}$ead the story of the unforgiving servant in Matthew 18:23–35. What does it teach us about forgiveness? How might it speak in your situation?

_____

_____

_____

_____

_____

_____

_____

_____

_____

_____

_____

_____

_____

_____

_____

_____

_____

_____

Read the Bible verses concerning forgiveness listed in the Appendix. Now write what God is revealing to you through them.

_____

_____

_____

_____

_____

_____

_____

_____

_____

_____

_____

_____

_____

_____

_____

_____

_____

_____

_____

DAY 12

～

"And be kind to one another, tenderhearted, forgiving one another, even as God in Christ forgave you" (Ephesians 4:32). We are commanded to forgive like Jesus. What does that mean? Describe how Jesus forgave you. (For example: unconditionally, willingly.)

_____

_____

_____

_____

_____

_____

_____

_____

_____

_____

_____

_____

_____

_____

_____

_____

_____

_____

DAY 13

*C*hoosing to forgive is an act of your will. It is not based on your feelings. What feelings have been holding you back from forgiving your offender(s)?

_____

_____

_____

_____

_____

_____

_____

_____

_____

_____

_____

_____

_____

_____

_____

_____

_____

_____

_____

Will you make the decision to forgive your offender(s) today? If not, why are you choosing to stay in the prison of unforgiveness, instead?

_____

_____

_____

_____

_____

_____

_____

_____

_____

_____

_____

_____

_____

_____

_____

_____

_____

_____

_____

_____

DAY 14

hen you don't forgive, you end up being tormented and imprisoned by your unforgiveness. God commands us to forgive. He gave us the four keys to freedom. Use this forgiveness prayer key to break free from *that moment*:

Heavenly Father, I choose to forgive (name the person who offended you) for what he/she did to me. (Be specific and name the offense—look at your entry on Day 5.) I believe the blood of Jesus covers that person's sin.

After you pray, use a red marker and mark out everything you listed on Day 5. This represents the blood of Jesus covering this offense against you.

Are there others you need to forgive? If so, list them and what they did or didn't do to hurt you. (The list may include parents, siblings, friends, teachers, bosses, coworkers, spouse, or children). Use today's key to forgive the people on this list.

_____

_____

_____

_____

_____

_____

_____

_____

_____

_____

DAY 15

se this prayer key to forgive the offender for the painful feelings you have experienced as a result of *that moment*:

I choose to forgive him/her for the feelings that I experienced because of the offense. (Be specific and list the emotions you experienced—look at your entry on Day 6.) I believe the blood of Jesus covers all of these emotions.

After you pray, use a red marker and mark out each feeling you listed on Day 6. This represents the blood of Jesus covering those feelings.

List any additional feelings you have experienced due to the offenses of others. (Look at the people you listed on Day 14, and look at the List of Feelings in the Appendix to identify all the emotions.) Use today's key to forgive the hurtful emotions on this list.

_____

_____

_____

_____

_____

_____

_____

_____

_____

_____

_____

DAY 16

Use this prayer key to forgive the negative effects of *that moment* on the other areas of your life:

I choose to forgive him (or her) for the domino effect caused by the offense. (List all of them—look at your entry on Day 7.) I believe the blood of Jesus covers all of these ramifications.

After you pray, use a red marker and mark out everything you listed on Day 7. This represents the blood of Jesus covering all of the ramifications of *that moment*.

Look at the people you listed on Day 14. List any additional ramifications you have experienced because of their offenses. Use today's key to forgive the ramifications on this list.

_____

_____

_____

_____

_____

_____

_____

_____

_____

_____

_____

DAY 17

$\mathcal{U}$se this final prayer key to complete the process of allowing forgiveness to set you free. It is confessing and repenting of your sinful reactions to *that moment*:

Lord, I acknowledge that I have sinned, too. I confess my sinful reactions. (Be specific—look at your entry on Day 8.) Thank you that the blood of Jesus covers my sins and that I am forgiven.

After you pray, use a red marker and mark out all of your sinful reactions listed on Day 8. This represents the blood of Jesus covering those sins.

Are there more sinful reactions you need to confess? If so, list them. Use today's key to repent of your sinful reactions toward others.

_____

_____

_____

_____

_____

_____

_____

_____

_____

_____

_____

_____

What has God shown you throughout the process of forgiving others?

_____

_____

_____

_____

_____

_____

_____

_____

_____

_____

_____

_____

_____

_____

_____

_____

_____

_____

_____

DAY 18

*I*f you want to make sure you have forgiven your offenders truly and completely, ask yourself if you can do the following:

1. Can you talk about this experience or person without getting angry, without feeling resentful, and without the slightest thought of revenge?

2. Can you revisit the scene or the person(s) involved without experiencing a negative reaction?

3. Have you been able to thank God for the lessons learned through the offense (1 Thessalonians 5:16–18, Ephesians 5:20)?

4. Are you willing to reward with good those who have hurt you (Romans 12:21)?

Did you answer "no" to any of these questions? Explain. You may need to revisit extending forgiveness so you can be totally free.

_____

_____

_____

_____

_____

_____

_____

_____

_____

_____

DAY 19

〜

"Therefore if you bring your gift to the altar, and there remember that your brother has something against you, leave your gift there before the altar, and go your way. First be reconciled to your brother, and then come and offer your gift" (Matthew 5:23–24).

Asking people to forgive you after you hurt them requires first being willing to admit and take full responsibility for what you said or did that offended them. Don't blame others or try to excuse yourself.

If possible, go to that person or call (avoid writing a letter, emailing, or texting). This needs to be a personal apology. Be willing to look that person in the eye and say, "I was wrong for (list what you said or did). Would you please forgive me?"

Who is the person you need to go to and seek forgiveness? How did you hurt that person?

_____

_____

_____

_____

_____

_____

_____

_____

_____

_____

_____

_____

_____

_____

_____

_____

_____

_____

_____

_____

_____

_____

_____

_____

_____

_____

_____

_____

_____

_____

_____

_____

_____

Pray for a good time to go and seek forgiveness.

DAY 20

Have you been blaming God for the painful experiences you or someone else has gone through? Are you angry with Him? Because God is good and righteous, you don't need to forgive Him. He never does anything wrong. If you have been judging God, repent today.

Read through the list "God's Character Traits" in the Appendix. Write the qualities that stand out to you and explain why you chose them.

_____

_____

_____

_____

_____

_____

_____

_____

_____

_____

_____

_____

_____

_____

_____

_____

DAY 21

⁓

*A*re you struggling with regret and shame? It's not a matter of forgiving yourself; it's a matter of receiving God's forgiveness and repenting of self-judgment. You could pray something like the following:

Heavenly Father, I confess I've been judging myself and holding myself guilty. I repent of judging myself and competing with You. You are God and I am not. Thank you for forgiving all of my sins and failures. This day, I receive Your total forgiveness. In Jesus' name. Amen.

Write how God touched your life through this book, *Grace Letters: Practical Steps to Experiencing Transformation through Forgiveness*, at my email, livinghopepub@yahoo.com.

Send me your picture and your forgiveness story so I can add you to my Freedom Wall! Or, if you are still struggling, write and tell me. I will try to help you.

_____

_____

_____

_____

_____

_____

_____

_____

_____

_____

FORGIVENESS SCRIPTURES

God's Forgiveness

"And according to the law almost all things are purified with blood, and without shedding of blood there is no remission [forgiveness]" (Hebrews 9:22).

"The next day John saw Jesus coming toward him, and said, 'Behold! The Lamb of God who takes away the sin of the world!'" (John 1:29).

"[Jesus] in whom we have redemption [salvation, freedom, deliverance] through His blood, the forgiveness of sins" (Colossians 1:14).

"All we like sheep have gone astray; we have turned, every one, to his own way; and the Lord has laid on Him the iniquity [sin] of us all" (Isaiah 53:6).

Forgiving Those Who Have Hurt You

"And whenever you stand praying, if you have anything against anyone, forgive him, that your Father in heaven may also forgive you your trespasses [offense, sin, wrong]" (Mark 11:25).

"For if you forgive men their trespasses [unlawful acts causing injury to the person, property, or rights of another], your heavenly Father will also forgive you" (Matthew 6:14).

"Bearing with one another, and forgiving one another, if anyone has a complaint against another; even as Christ forgave you, so you also must do" (Colossians 3:13).

"And be kind to one another, tenderhearted, forgiving one another, even as God in Christ forgave you" (Ephesians 4:32).

"Then his master, after he had called him, said to him, 'You wicked servant! I forgave you all that debt because you begged me. Should you not also have had compassion on your fellow servant, just as I had pity on you?' And his master was angry, and delivered him to the torturers until he should pay all that was due to him. So My heavenly Father also will do to you if each of you, from his heart, does not forgive his brother his trespasses" (Matthew 18:32–35).

"Then Peter came to Him and said, 'Lord, how often shall my brother sin against me, and I forgive him? Up to seven times?' Jesus said to him, 'I do not say to you, up to seven times, but up to seventy times seven'" (Matthew 18:21–22).

Asking Those You Have Hurt to Forgive You

"Therefore if you bring your gift to the altar, and there remember that your brother has something against you, leave your gift there before the altar, and go your way. First be reconciled to your brother, and then come and offer your gift" (Matthew 5:23–24).

"If it is possible, as much as depends on you, live peaceably with all men" (Romans 12:18).

LIST OF FEELINGS

abandoned
accepted
afraid
ambivalent
angry
anxious
ashamed
awkward
belittled
betrayed
bewildered
bitter
bored
bothered
broken
burdened
cheated
coerced
competitive
concerned
condemned
confused
controlled

crushed
cynical
deceived
defeated
defensive
depressed
desperate
destructive
determined
devastated
disappointed
discouraged
disgraced
disgusted
dismayed
distant
eager
embarrassed
empty
exhausted
fearful
flustered
foolish

frantic
frustrated
furious
greedy
grief
guilty
harassed
hated
hateful
helpless
hopeless
horrible
horrified
humiliated
hurt
hysterical
ignored
impatient
imposed upon
inadequate
infatuated
infuriated
insecure

intimidated
irritated
isolated
jealous
judged
jumpy
justified
lazy
left out
let down
lonely
lost
low
mad
manipulated
mean
miserable
misunderstood
neglected
nervous
obsessed
offended
outraged

overwhelmed	ridiculed	tense	unloved
panicked	sad	terrible	unorganized
peeved	screwed up	terrified	unsettled
persecuted	shame	threatened	unwanted
pitiful	shocked	timid	upset
pressured	shy	tired	uptight
proud	skeptical	tormented	used
puzzled	smothered	torn	vindictive
quarrelsome	sorry	trapped	violent
quiet	spiteful	troubled	vulnerable
rage	stressed	ugly	weary
rebellious	stunned	unaccepted	weepy
rejected	stupid	unappreciated	wicked
reluctant	surprised	uncomfortable	worried
resentful	suspicious	undecided	worthless
resigned	tearful	uneasy	wounded
restless	tempted	unhappy	wronged

GOD'S CHARACTER TRAITS

Faithful

God will always do what He has said and fulfill what He has promised. "God is not a man, that He should lie, Nor a son of man, that He should repent. Has He said, and will He not do? Or has He spoken, and will He not make it good?" (Numbers 23:19).

Good

All that God is and does is worthy of approval, and He is the final standard of goodness. "The Lord is good, A stronghold in the day of trouble; And He knows those who trust in Him" (Nahum 1:7).

Love

God is freely and eternally giving of Himself for the good of others. "He who does not love does not know God, for God is love" (1 John 4:8).

Merciful

God is kind toward those in misery and distress. "And David said to Gad, 'I am in great distress. Please let us fall into the hand of the Lord, for His mercies are great; but do not let me fall into the hand of man'" (2 Samuel 24:14).

Gracious

God offers kindness toward those who deserve only punishment. "For He says to Moses, 'I will have mercy on whomever I will have mercy, and I will have compassion on whomever I will have compassion'" (Romans 9:15).

Patient

God offers kindness in withholding punishment of those who sin, even over a period of time. "And the Lord passed before him [Moses] and proclaimed, 'The Lord, the Lord God, merciful and gracious, longsuffering, and abounding in goodness and truth'" (Exodus 34:6).

Holy

God is separated from sin, and He is not evil. "And one cried to another and said: 'Holy, holy, holy is the Lord of hosts; the whole earth is full of His glory!'" (Isaiah 6:3).

God of Peace

In God's being and actions, He is separate from all confusion and disorder, yet He is continually active in innumerable well-ordered, fully controlled, and simultaneous actions. "For God is not the author of confusion but of peace, as in all the churches of the saints" (1 Corinthians 14:33).

Righteous (Just)

God always acts in accordance with what is right, and He is the final standard of what is right. "He is the Rock, His work is perfect; for all His ways are justice, a God of truth and without injustice; righteous and upright is He" (Deuteronomy 32:4).

ABOUT THE AUTHOR

⁓

Dr. Emily Edwards is an emerging voice of hope within the field of Christian counseling. She is a bright, positive, and informed writer and speaker who spends much of her time counseling and helping others in the pursuit, development, and implementation of long-term, meaningful relationships. She frequently travels around the United States and overseas, leading seminars and retreats for singles, women, and married couples. Edwards received her Ph.D. in Christian Counseling from Vision International University in 2002, along with certifications in pastoral counseling and marriage and family counseling. In 2015, Edwards received her master's in biblical counseling from Victorious Christian Life Institute. The scope of her work and ministry includes personal counseling, teaching biblical principles on relationships, forgiveness, and recovery for the hurting.

CPSIA information can be obtained
at www.ICGtesting.com
Printed in the USA
LVHW021211150723
752517LV00012B/1389